AF249190

35
mf
5 2 1 3
5 2 1 3
38
8va---
mp
3
3
4
41
5
5 1 3
44
5 1
5 1 3
47
4
1 3

The Blended Service

10 Inspiring Arrangements of Praise Songs with Hymns

Arranged by Alex-Zsolt

"Let the message of Christ dwell among you richly as you teach and admonish one another with all wisdom through psalms, hymns, and songs from the Spirit, singing to God with gratitude in your hearts."
Colossians 3:16

The scripture above was heavy on my heart when choosing and creating the selections in this book, *The Blended Service.* Today, many churches worship through a blend of music that can be found in a single service or two separate services. Some churches have separate services that focus on each style of music, traditional or contemporary. After writing *The Traditional Service* and *The Contemporary Service*, it seemed appropriate to create a book that combined both styles of worship. I really enjoyed arranging the music in this book that brings together hymns and praise songs. Each selection is a medley that has a common theme. I chose music that had similar titles between the hymns and praise songs and lyrics that shared the same message for the sole purpose of blending each style of worship in unity. This is why the scripture above is the foundation of this book. The prayer for all of us is to have wisdom through psalms, hymns, and songs from the Spirit so that we can sing or play to God with gratitude in our hearts.

Produced by
Alfred Music
P.O. Box 10003
Van Nuys, CA 91410-0003
alfred.com

Printed in USA.

ISBN-10: 0-7390-9869-1
ISBN-13: 978-0-7390-9869-1

Cover Photos:
Modern white church steeple with cross: © Shutterstock / Patrick Poendl • church: © Shutterstock / Birton

Blessed Be Your Name
with
Blessed Be the Name

Words and Music by
Beth Redman and Matt Redman
Arr. Alex-Zsolt

65
f
69
mf
73
mf
77
"Blessed Be the Name"
Traditional Hymn
f
81

85
89
ff
93
ff
A little slower (♩ = 108)
97
mf
dim. poco a poco
101
p
rit.

(*Approx. Performance Time – 4:15*)

Breathe
with
Breathe on Me, Breath of God

Words and Music by Marie Barnett
Arr. Alex-Zsolt

"Breathe on Me, Breath of God"
Edwin Hatch

Draw Me Close
with
Draw Me Nearer

Words and Music by Kelly Carpenter
Arr. Alex-Zsolt

Slower (♩= 80)
12
mp
15
18
mf
21
cresc. poco a poco
24
Faster (♩= 96)
accel.
f

Slower (= 80)
mp
p
"Draw Me Nearer"
Words by Fanny Crosby
Music by W. Howard Doane
mp

41
rit.
44
Faster (♩ = 84)
mf
48
3
52
8va
a tempo
rit.
accel.
mp
3
5
56
rit. poco a poco
mf
mp
p
8va

(Approx. Performance Time — 4:00)

Holy Is the Lord
with
Holy, Holy, Holy

Words and Music by
Chris Tomlin and Louie Giglio
Arr. Alex-Zsolt

With awe (♩ = 84)

"Holy, Holy, Holy"
Words by Reginald Heber
Music by John B. Dykes

a tempo
14
mp
18
dim. poco a poco
22
a tempo
8va--
rit.
p
f
mf
26
29
* Glissando on white keys

cresc. poco a poco
ff

65
mf
5 2 1 2
5 2 1 2
69
mp
4 1
3 1
2
4 1
5 2 1 2
5
73
4 1
3 1
5 2
5 2 1
1
4
mf
1 2
77
4 1
mp
81
cresc. poco a poco
3 1
5 2
poco rit.
f
p

Friend of God
with
What a Friend We Have in Jesus

Words and Music by
Israel Houghton and Michael Gungor
Arr. Alex-Zsolt

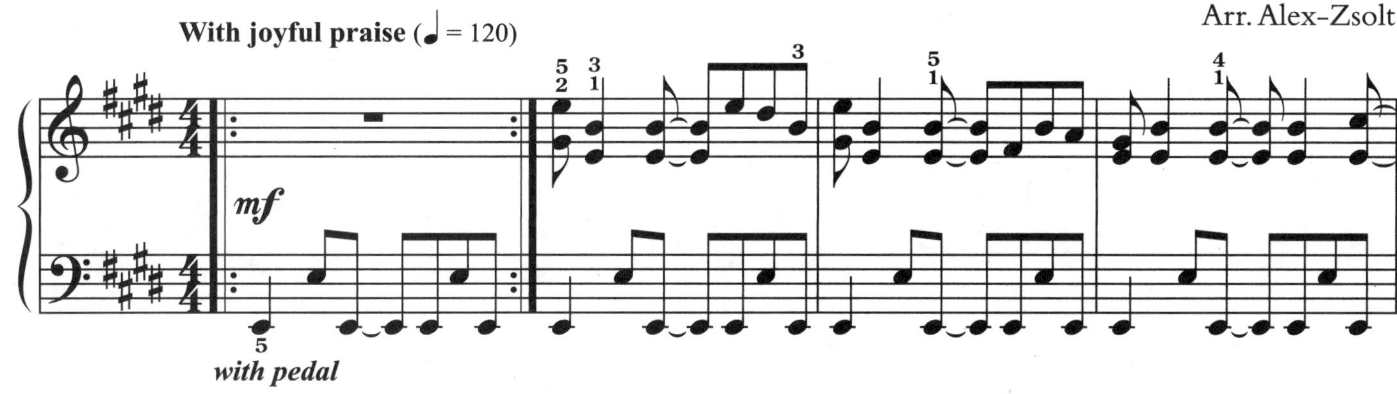

37
41
45
49
53
f
ff
mp
dim. poco a poco
cresc. poco a poco

mf
cresc. poco a poco
Slower (♩ = 76)
Freely (♩ = 72)
"What a Friend We Have in Jesus"
Words by Joseph M. Scriven
Music by Charles C. Converse
mf
mp
p

How Deep the Father's Love for Us
with
My Savior's Love

Words and Music by Stuart Townend
Arr. Alex-Zsolt

a tempo
14
mp
17
mf
20
f
mf
23
1
f
25
2 1 2
5
mf
f
5 2 1 4 3 2 1 2

"My Savior's Love"
Charles H. Gabriel
a tempo
rit.
mp
mf
mp
cresc. poco a poco
f

Above All
with
Jesus Paid It All

Words and Music by
Paul Baloche and Lenny LeBlanc
Arr. Alex-Zsolt

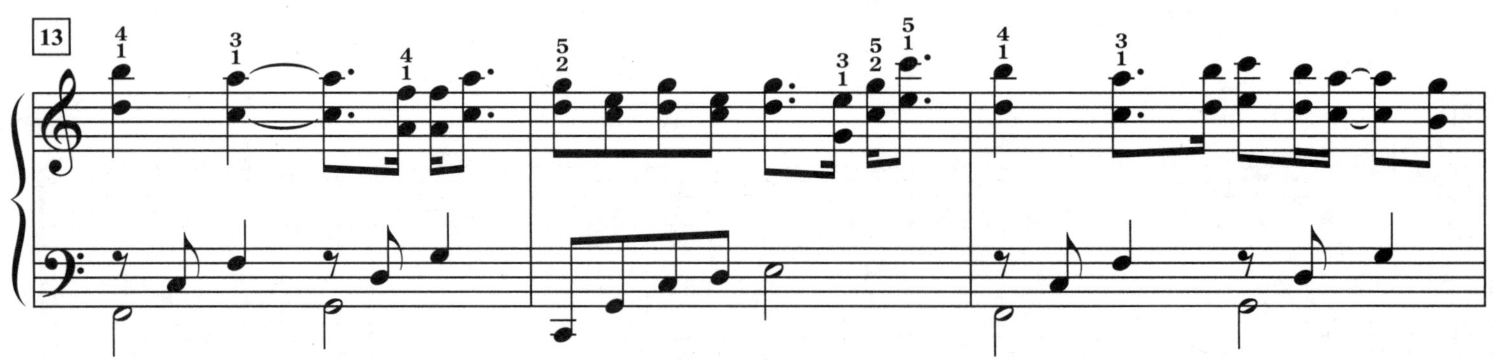

mf
f
mf
mp
p
cresc. poco a poco
molto rit.

a tempo
ff
f
A little faster (= 80)
"Jesus Paid It All"
Words by Elvina M. Hall
Music by John T. Grape
mf
mp
mel.
mf

52
mel.
a tempo
mf
freely
f
56
mf
f
60
freely
64
a tempo
ff
mf
68
mp
rit.
p
8va

(Approx. Performance Time – 2:45)

Sing, Sing, Sing
with
I Sing the Mighty Power of God

Words and Music by Chris Tomlin,
Daniel Carson, Jesse Reeves, Matt Gilder and Travis Nunn
Arr. Alex-Zsolt

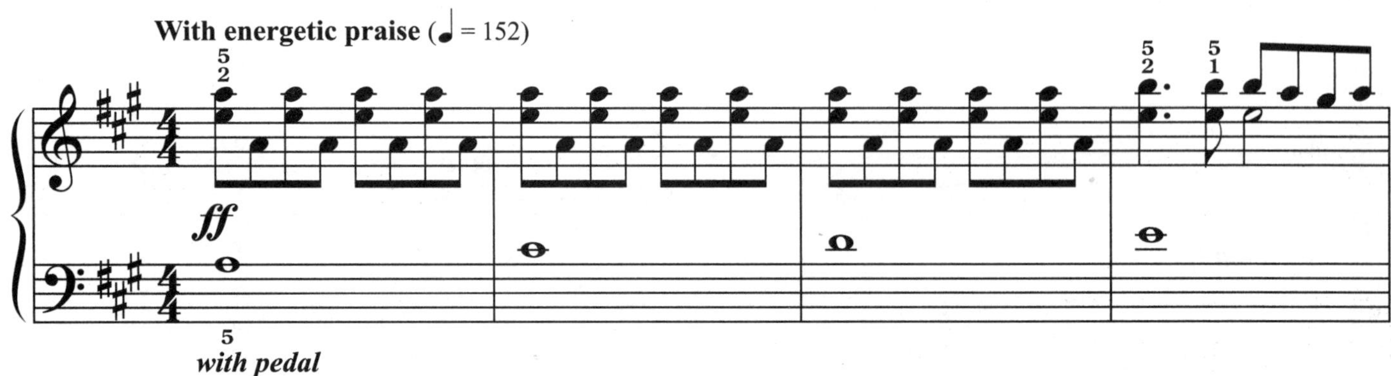

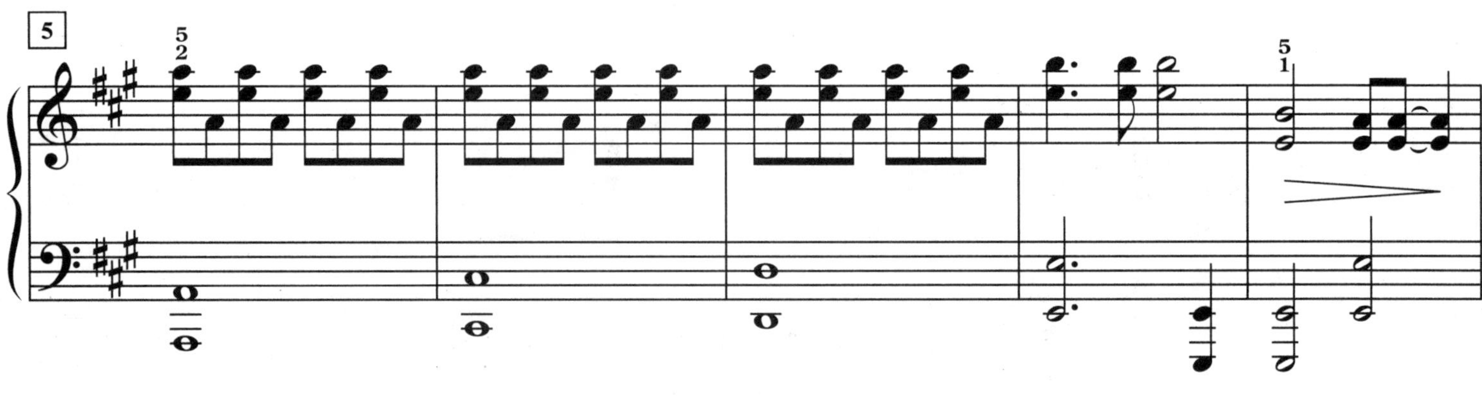

18
(8va)
22
25
28
32
* Glissando on white keys

“I Sing the Mighty Power of God”
Issac Watts

56
mf
59
Slower (♩ = 80)
rit.
mf
62
Faster (♩ = 152)
mp
p
65
ff
Majestic (♩ = 132)
68
8va

72
76
Slower
(= 100)
mf
rit.
8va
80
5
5 2 1 2
3
84
3
1
4
2
2/4
4/4
f poco a poco dim. e rit.
5 2
1
4
5
88
a tempo
mf
f
5 2
5 1 4

I Give You My Heart
with
Near to the Heart of God

Words and Music by Reuben Morgan
Arr. Alex-Zsolt

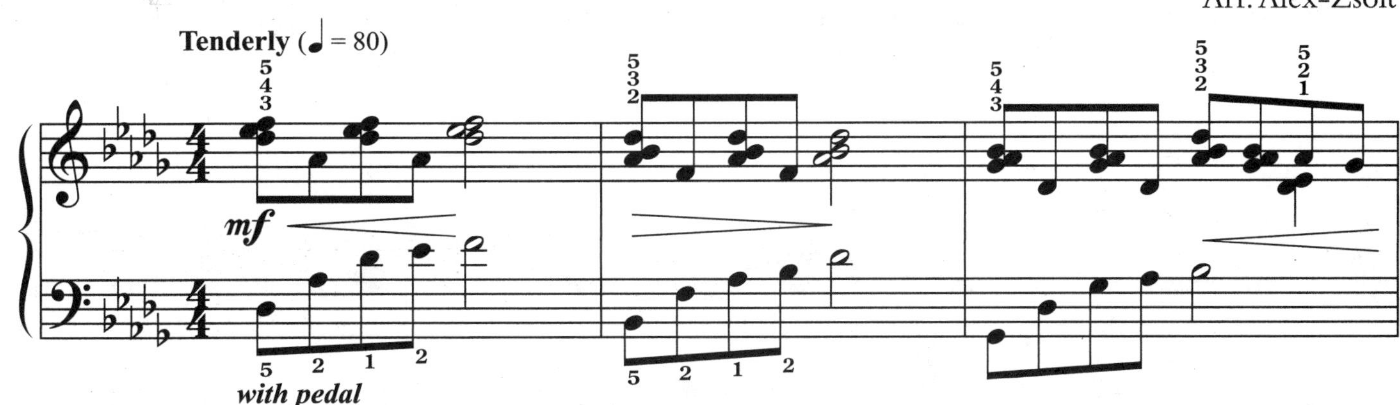

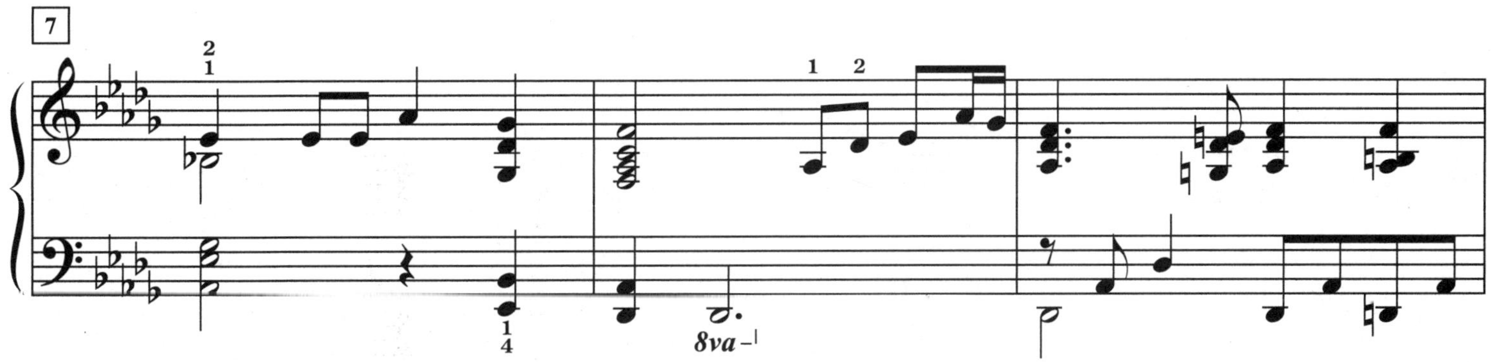

13
16
19
22
"I Give You My Heart"
Words and Music by Reuben Morgan
26

49
mf
mf
52
8va –
55
58
A little faster (♩ = 84)
f
mf
61
ff

64
67
70
73
77
f
ff
mf
mp
a tempo
rit.
rit.
mp
8va
5
1
1
2
5
2
5
2
1
1
1
1
1
5
3
2
1
3
2
1

(*Approx. Performance Time – 3:00*)

A New Hallelujah
with
Hallelujah! Thine the Glory

Words and Music by
Deborah Smith, Michael W. Smith and Paul Baloche

Arr. Alex-Zsolt

60
ff
mf
63
67
cresc. poco a poco
71
f
dim. poco a poco
76
mp